F is for **Football**

Ned Elliott
Charles C Somerville

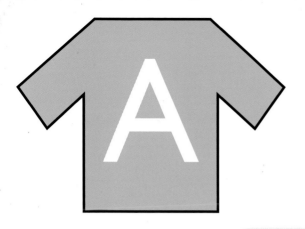

Association Football

Association Football is the official name of the game, which distinguishes it from other types of football – Rugby Football, American Football, Aussie Rules and Gaelic Football among others. "As**soc**iation" is where the name "**soc**cer" comes from, but many people call it simply "football".

The Football Association (FA) was formed in London in 1863 to create a common set of rules (as had been done for cricket). Until then, different versions of the game were played across the country. This caused problems when teams from different areas played each other – such as clubs fielding a different number of players.

Come on lads! Only eleven of them turned up!

Call this football?

Some teams played rougher than others, allowing players to kick, and even sit on, the opposition. One player at Westminster School described how his team mates would do "anything short of **MURDER** to get the ball".

I'm forever blowing bubbles, Pretty bubbles in the air ... I'm forever blowing bubbles, Pretty bubbles in the air. They fly so high, nearly reach the sky. Then like my dreams they fade and die. Fortune's always hiding, I've looked everywhere, I'm forever blowing bubbles, Pretty bubbles in the air ...

Anthem

Chanting and singing by football supporters is a feature of all big football matches, whether it's *You'll never walk alone*, sung by the Liverpool crowd, *One-nil to the Arsenal*, or the many versions of *Olé, Olé, Olé*, chanted by fans across the world.

West Ham United was one of the first clubs to adopt its own anthem with *I'm Forever Blowing Bubbles* in the 1920s. In 1999, before a home match against Middlesbrough, 23,680 supporters blew bubbles for one minute to get into the *Guinness Book of Records*. Not only did the club set a new world record off the pitch, but it also won 4-0 on it.

All-rounders

Charles Burgess Fry (CB Fry) was one of the greatest sporting all-rounders. He played football for England and reached the final of the FA Cup with Southampton in 1902. He played rugby for the Barbarians and in 1893 equalled the world record for the long jump. CB Fry was also England's cricket captain and scored a record six first-class centuries in a row in 1901. But perhaps best of all, his party piece was to jump backwards onto a mantelpiece.
[Don't try this at home!]

Balls

Footballs were painted with a black and white chequered effect to make them stand out on black and white television during the 1970 World Cup. Now we have colour televisions, footballs come in **bright colours** to match.

Thank goodness, for one moment I thought it was a head!

The oldest known football is more than 450 years old and was found hidden in the rafters above Mary Queen of Scots' bedroom in Stirling Castle. Perhaps it belonged to her great-uncle, Henry VIII. We know that he enjoyed a kick about as his royal football boots were listed in the "Great Wardrobe" of 1526.

Rule(r)s of the game

Boots

In the 1800s, players wore their hard, thick leather work boots, with steel toe-caps, as the first football boots. These had metal studs or tacks put in the sole to stop players sliding on the pitch. By the end of that century, the first specially designed football boots appeared, which covered the ankle for increased protection from crunching tackles. Today, with stricter rules to stop players from getting hurt, boots are becoming more like ballet shoes. And they come in all shades and colours too.

Ball skills

Juggling (or "keepy-uppies") involves keeping the ball off the ground by using any part of the body except the hands and arms. It's difficult to do, but is a good way to improve your ball skills.

The record for "the longest distance travelled while juggling a football" is held by Dan Magness. He walked 320 kilometres from London to Manchester while keeping a ball in the air, doing around half a million keepy-uppies over his 10-day journey.

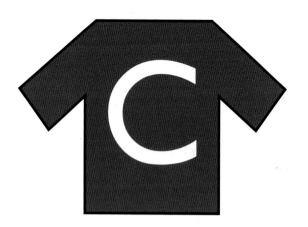

Cuju

According to FIFA, cuju (meaning "kick ball") is the earliest form of football, originating in China in the 3rd century BC. It involved kicking a leather ball through a small hole in a piece of silk cloth, which was fixed onto bamboo canes and hung about nine metres above ground.

Club

Dublin University Football Club, in the Republic of Ireland, was founded in 1854 and claims to be the oldest "football" club in the world. However, the Club now plays Rugby Union, so both the FA and FIFA recognise Sheffield Football Club as being the oldest, which began in England in 1857, just three years later.

Cup

The oldest football competition is the FA Cup, which kicked off in 1871. It's a knock-out competition between English clubs, with more than 700 now taking part. The final is played at London's Wembley Stadium.

While there are many competitions played between clubs, the World Cup is a tournament played between international teams every four years.

Just days before the 1966 World Cup, the winner's trophy was stolen. Fortunately, a dog named Pickles came to the rescue and discovered it a week later, wrapped in newspaper under a garden hedge in South London. Pickles became a celebrity – he starred in a feature film, appeared on several television shows and was made Dog of the Year.

In 1970, Brazil was allowed to keep the Cup forever, after winning it for a third time, but in 1983 it was stolen again and never recovered. The new World Cup isn't a cup at all – it's a gold trophy, which shows two human figures holding up the Earth.

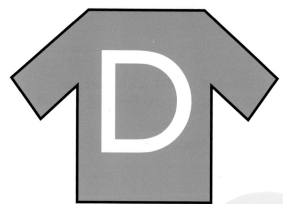

Derby

To many people, Derby is just another town in the English Midlands, but to football fans it marks one of the most exciting days in the footballing calendar. That's because a "derby" is a match played between two local teams and a chance to get one over your biggest rival. Famous rivalries include the Old Firm (Rangers and Celtic in Glasgow), the Mersey Derby (Liverpool and Everton), the Derby della Madonnina (AC Milan and Inter Milan) and many more.

Why "derby"? The term is thought to come from the rivalry between two church teams (St Peter's and All Saints) in Derby in the mid-1800s.

Diving

Some footballers will try to win free kicks and get their opponents sent off by diving on the floor and pretending to be fouled.

Chilean player Bryan Carrasco went even further by grabbing his opponent's hand and punching himself in the face during a match. Amazingly, the ploy worked and the referee awarded Chile a free kick. While he "took one on the chin" for the Chileans, justice was done as his team lost the match.

Defence

Players will stand together to form a wall to defend against a free kick. The aim is to block the ball when it is kicked towards the goal. The ball is kicked very hard so the players will try to protect themselves.

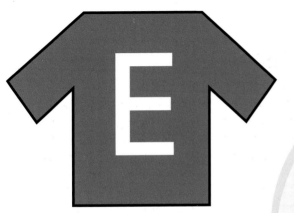

Extra time

In a league competition, both teams will be awarded one point if the match ends in a draw. However, in a knock-out cup competition, only one team will go through to the next round, so a winner needs to be found.

If scores are level at the end of 90 minutes, then 30 minutes of extra time will be played. And if the match is still level after that? Then there is either a replay or the **DREADED PENALTY SHOOT-OUT**.

11 Eleven

It is thought that football teams have 11 players because in the 19th century, when modern football began, dormitories at English boarding schools had ten pupils. Early games were often played by one dormitory against another – so 10 pupils, plus the teacher, made 11 in each team.

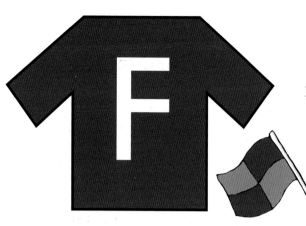

Fans

Big European football clubs have support around the world. The world's biggest club, Manchester United, claims to have 650 million fans (more than the population of Europe).

FIFA

FIFA, the international football governing body, was set up in 1904 by eight football associations to help spread the game across the world. Now, with 209 members (more than the United Nations), football is truly a world game. Nations that are not part of FIFA include: Monaco (which plays in the French league), the Vatican City (which is too busy praying), and the United Kingdom (which is represented by England, Scotland, Northern Ireland and Wales).

The **loudest** fans belong to the Turkish side Galatasaray. In March 2011, in a derby against Fenerbahçe in Istanbul, noise levels reached more than 131 decibels – the same as listening to a jet engine 30 metres away. In comparison, fans at Old Trafford (Manchester United's ground) have only reached 94 decibels (but still a level that could result in hearing loss).

Perhaps the popular chant "You're not singing anymore!" (targeted at opposing fans) should just be: "We can't hear you anymore!".

In 1993, Congleton Town called off a minute's silence to mourn the death of its oldest fan when he walked into the football ground ...

Who's the stiff?

Goals

One of the greatest ever football managers, Brian Clough, famously said, "It only takes a second to score a goal." However, this depends on where you're standing. The fastest goal from the kick-off took 2.8 seconds and was scored by Uruguay's Ricardo Oliveira in 1998, who shot the ball from the half-way line. His nickname was "Chispero" or "Spark plug".

Hang on! I'm the one who scored!

Goal celebration

Goal celebrations have certainly changed over the years. In the 1950s and 1960s, they comprised nothing more than a firm handshake with a team mate and possibly a pat on the back. Later, players threw their arms in the air and jumped for joy. Nowadays, a goal can prompt not just kissing and cuddling, but the start of a choreographed routine and an elaborate gymnastics display.

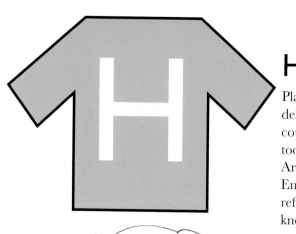

Hand of God

Players are not allowed to handle the ball deliberately (unless you are the goalkeeper of course). The most notorious handball incident took place during the 1986 World Cup, when Argentina's Diego Maradona played against England in the quarter finals. Unseen by the referee, he punched the ball into the net to knock England out. His excuse? It wasn't him, it was the "hand of God".

Perhaps God was on his side as, despite being a cheat, Maradona went on in the same match to score one of the best goals in football history and later to hold aloft the World Cup as captain that year.

Half-time

"It's a game of two halves." Today, teams change ends at half-time, but this wasn't always the case – the 1863 football rules stated that sides must change ends after every goal scored.

Hat-trick

A "hat-trick" is when a player scores three goals in a single match. The term comes from cricket (where it is used to describe bowling three players out in a row). In 1966, Geoff Hurst scored the first ever hat-trick in a World Cup final to help England win the trophy for the first time.

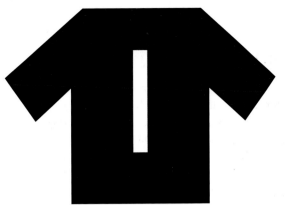

Injury

Alex Stepney was Manchester United's goalkeeper, who helped win the European Cup in 1968. He became so animated during a League match in 1975 shouting at his own defenders that he dislocated his jaw and had to be taken to hospital.

Internationals

The first international game was played in London in March 1870 between England and Scotland, but as both teams were selected by the FA, no born-and-bred Scottish players took part.

Bert Trautmann, Manchester City's German goalie, played more than 15 minutes of the 1956 FA Cup Final at Wembley after breaking his neck. During that time, he made crucial saves to secure his team's victory. Bert shook hands with the Queen as he collected his winner's medal from the Royal Box, but he needed his other hand to hold his head up straight.

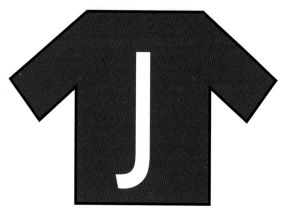

Jumpers for goalposts

"Jumpers for goalposts" have been used by generations of children to play football on the street, in the park, in the playground, on the beach – pretty much anywhere. (Note to anyone planning to visit the UK – yes, you do need to take jumpers to the beach.)

Jackets

Until the 1950s, referees usually wore a black jacket or blazer and the tradition of wearing black continues today. Referees wear black shirts, shorts, socks and football boots.

Since the 1994 World Cup finals, referees have been allowed to wear red, yellow, green and blue, in addition to the traditional black shirt, for international matches.

Kit

It was only in 1870 that the first football kits were worn, and colours used to represent each team. When the FA was established in 1863, football players didn't wear specific kits, but instead wore caps or scarves to show which team they belonged to. Each time a player represented England, he was awarded an international cap (made of white silk with a red rose embroidered on the front). While players no longer wear caps on the pitch, the term "cap" is used to indicate international appearances.

Before 1913, goalkeepers wore the same kit as everyone else in the team. Today, they wear different coloured shirts. Why? To make it easier for the referee to see whether a defender handles the ball instead of the goalkeeper.

Keeper

Nothing could get past goalkeeper William "Fatty" Foulke, who was 1.93 metres tall and weighed 22 stone. He played more than 400 matches for Sheffield United, Chelsea and Bradford City between 1894 and 1907. He helped Sheffield United win the League and two FA Cups, and even played for England.

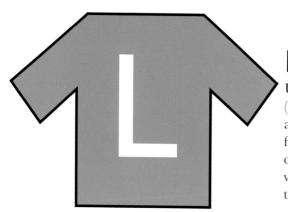

League

Unlike a cup competition (where half the teams are knocked out in the first round), a league competition gives even the worst team the opportunity to play week in, week out.

The "Football League", founded in 1888 as a competition for clubs in England and Wales, is the oldest such competition in the world. All the teams play each other twice in the season and are awarded three points for winning a match and one point for a draw. The team with the most points at the end of the season is the League Champion.

In 1992, the clubs in the first division of the Football League split away to form a separate Premier League.

Scilly by name, silly by nature – the smallest football league in the world is on the Isles of Scilly. It has two clubs, Woolpack Wanderers and Garrison Gunners, which play each other about 20 times a season. They compete for two Scilly cups too.

Linesmen

Linesmen (sometimes called referee's assistants) help the referee by indicating when the ball has gone out of play and with offside decisions.

The linesman is flagging!

WHEEZE GASP COUGH

Mascots

"Cyril the Swan", the giant feathered mascot of Swansea City, was banned from the pitch and fined £1,000 during a 1999 match against Norwich City, when he celebrated a goal with a pitch-invading dance.

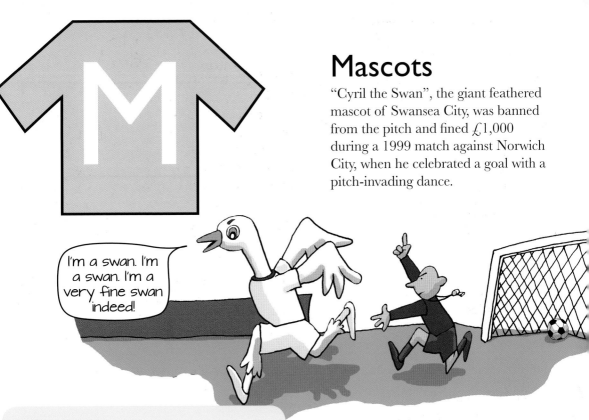

I'm a swan. I'm a swan. I'm a very fine swan indeed!

Mishap

There was a bit of a diplomatic incident after the Czech Republic played a friendly in Prague in May 2008. The match-day programme included the Latvian team picture, with all the right names printed alongside, and the Latvian flag, with all the right colours. There was a perfect rendition of the Latvian national anthem before the match. But the Czech team was playing Lithuania!

Bradford City's mascot is the "City Gent" – a rather tubby figure, who wears a bowler hat. Lenny Berry dressed up as the City Gent for nearly 20 years, but was forced to quit after he lost weight! A bit tough for Lenny, but it's perhaps better to be a mascot than a manager – Bradford City saw off 17 of them during Lenny's time at the club.

"Man of the Match"

The player thought to have made the biggest contribution to a game is named "Man of the Match". Each season, the player voted by journalists, coaches and players as the best in the world is awarded FIFA's *Ballon d'Or* (Golden Ball).

You're fired!

Numbers

Numbers on the back of players' shirts help spectators and the referee to tell them apart.

The first time numbers were used in Europe was in August 1928, when Sheffield Wednesday played Arsenal and Chelsea hosted Swansea Town at Stamford Bridge. When the Chelsea team toured South America the following summer, it was given the nickname "*Los Numerados*" by the locals.

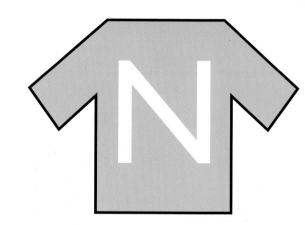

Net

Goal nets were not introduced until 1891. Before then, it wasn't always easy for the referee to tell whether the ball went inside, or outside, the post. This situation wasn't helped by spectators, who would stand along the edge of the pitch – sometimes stopping the ball going into the goal.

The idea for a net came from Everton fan and civil engineer John Alexander Brodie, after a wrongly disallowed goal robbed his team of a victory against Accrington in 1889.

Back of the net!

Under today's football rules, it's not necessary to use a net, but it can prove to be very useful.

That gets my goat!

Nutmeg

If your opponent rolls the ball through your legs, he or she will shout "nutmeg" to let you know you've been tricked.

Why? In the 19th century, unscrupulous exporters of nutmeg sold wooden replicas of the valuable spice instead of the real thing – if you were fool enough to fall for them. Over time, the word "nutmeg" became associated with anyone similarly tricked.

Odd balls

The earliest footballs were made from inflated animal bladders, although very early games might have been played with human heads. Skulls of Roman or Viking invaders were said to have been used at various sporting events. In the Middle Ages, a severed head was kicked about by the crowd following an execution.

The British also played a type of football where teams competed to kick the head of an animal around their fields. The winning team buried the head on its land, thereby guaranteeing a good harvest.

Own goal

The record for the highest ever scoreline was in a match played in Madagascar in 2002, which ended 149-0. As a protest against a bad refereeing decision, SOE l'Emyrne players scored 149 own goals.

In 1976, Aston Villa's Chris Nicholl scored all four goals in a first division match against Leicester City. The final score was 2-2.

Offside rule

Sorry, the offside rule is too complicated and there's not enough space to explain it here!

Penalty

Originally called the "kick of death", the penalty was introduced in 1891, following a suggestion by Irish goalkeeper William McCrum, who wanted to end the practice of players fouling opponents or handling the ball to stop a goal.

On Boxing Day 1924, Nottingham Forest was losing 0-1 at home to Bolton Wanderers when the team was awarded a penalty. Unfortunately, Forest's regular penalty-taker Harry Martin had been carried off injured to the changing rooms. The captain insisted that players carried poor Harry back onto the pitch. From a standing position, he took the penalty, scored, collapsed and was carried off again.

In the 1938 World Cup semi-finals, Italy was awarded a penalty against Brazil. While Giuseppe Meazza was preparing to take it, his shorts fell down. He quickly pulled them up and shot the ball past the Brazilian goalie, who was still laughing.

Postponement

A match will be postponed if it can't be played for any reason. A cup tie in Scotland in 1963 between Airdrie and Stranraer had to be rescheduled 33 times because of bad weather (it was the coldest winter in over 200 years). The same winter caused chaos to matches in England too – in the third round of the FA Cup, 16 of the 32 ties were called off 10 times or more and it took 66 days before the round was completed.

Penalty shoot-outs

In 1970, FIFA and UEFA introduced the penalty shoot-out. Before then, cup ties were decided by endless replays or the toss of a coin. In some matches, players had to go on playing until someone scored a goal. This meant that in 1946 Stockport and Doncaster Rovers played a cup match that lasted three hours and 23 minutes, setting a world record.

Qualification

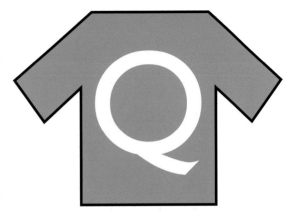

England and Scotland didn't qualify to play in the first ever World Cup in Uruguay in 1930, despite being (in their eyes at least) the best teams in the world. This was because they had withdrawn from FIFA following a dispute over payments and the amateur status of the game.

When England finally entered the competition in 1950, it was beaten 1-0 by the US, failing to get past the first round, in one of the most embarrassing defeats in team history.

It was widely reported that India didn't take part in the 1950 World Cup because players weren't allowed to play barefoot.

In 1954, Turkey knocked out Spain during a World Cup qualifier by drawing straws. Blindfolded Italian Luigi Franco Gemma picked the straws to decide the winner.

In 1992, Denmark won the European Championship, even though it had missed out on qualification. The Danes' unexpected inclusion was due to Yugoslavia dropping out of the tournament because the country had entered civil war. Denmark went on to win the whole thing, proving that you don't "have to be in it to win it"!

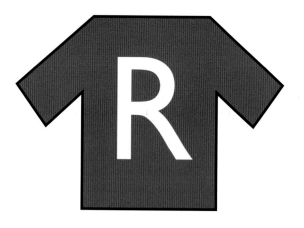

Relegation

At the end of the season, teams that have finished at the top of the league table (by winning lots of matches) might be promoted to a higher division. Equally, teams that have done badly (and haven't scored many points) might be relegated to play against teams that aren't so good. Clubs will go to extreme lengths to avoid relegation.

In 1957, the Salisbury and District FA of Rhodesia approved the payment of £10 for a witch doctor to perform magic spells to improve Salisbury's game. The team had lost every match the previous season.

The Sampdoria team was so relieved that it hadn't finished bottom of the Italian league table in 1969 that players walked 32 kilometres to a mountain sanctuary near Genoa to thank the Virgin Mary for helping them avoid relegation.

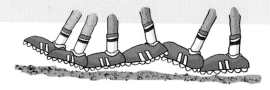

Referee

There was no referee in the original rules of the game. Instead, it was up to the captains of both sides to settle disputes. It was assumed that gentlemen would never intentionally foul. Today, decisions made by the referee are final.

In 1998, English referee Martin Sylvester sent himself off after punching a player during a game in the Andover and District Sunday League. However, if you think that his behaviour was unprofessional, a referee at a friendly match in Brazil drew a revolver and shot dead a player who had disputed a penalty decision. The referee escaped on horseback.

Referees need to be fit. Professional referees travel an average of 13 kilometres in a match – much of this distance will be run at full sprint.

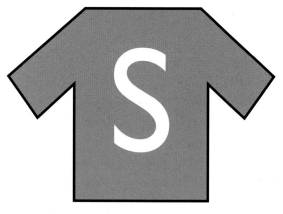

Striker

A striker is a centre forward who scores many goals. Kevin Keegan (known as "King Kev") was a star striker of the 1970s and was famous for captaining Newcastle and England, and going on to manage them both. However, what made him really stand out was his big bubble perm – a trend he set, which dominated football fashion for a decade!

Substitute

In 2004, James Hayter came on as an 84th-minute substitute for Bournemouth against Wrexham and scored the fastest Football League hat-trick ever. It took less than 140 seconds. Unfortunately, his family missed it. Assuming that James would not make an appearance, they left the match 10 minutes before the final whistle to catch a ferry back to their home on the Isle of Wight.

Stadium

Founded in 1875, Blackburn Rovers owes its name to its lowly beginnings. The team lacked an official ground in its early years so it was known simply as the "Rovers".

The biggest ever crowd at a football match watched Uruguay beat Brazil in the final game of the 1950 World Cup at the Maracana Stadium in Rio de Janeiro. Nearly 200,000 paid to watch, although 10,000 more were believed to have sneaked into the ground on the day.

Stoppage time

Stoppage time was introduced in 1891, after a match between Stoke City and Aston Villa. Trailing 1-0, and with just two minutes remaining, Stoke was awarded a penalty. Villa's goalkeeper kicked the ball out of the ground, and by the time it had been retrieved, the game was over. Stoppage time (for goal celebrations, substitutions, injury and deliberate stalling) is now added to each 45-minute half. Today, players who deliberately waste time are shown a yellow card.

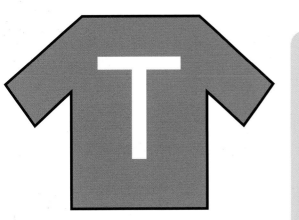

T

Transfers

Until the Football Association introduced player registration in 1885, there were no transfers – a player could agree to play one or more games for any football club at any time.

Now, the transfer of players is big business. Gareth Bale's transfer to Real Madrid in 2013 was the first to top €100 million.

Romanian midfielder Ion Radu was sold to Valcea in 1998 for two tonnes of pork and beef by second division Jiul Petrosani. "We will sell the meat, then pay all the other players' salaries," said the club president.

Throw in

When the ball goes off the side of the pitch, a player throws it back into play from the point it went off. The ball must be thrown with two hands, from behind the player's head, and both feet must be on the ground.

Throwing a tantrum

Throwing the ball in frustration isn't allowed – especially towards the referee! In 1986, Ray ("Butch") Wilkins did just that and became the first England player ever to be sent off at the World Cup finals. This red card was the first and last in his entire career, which spanned 25 years and nearly 800 games.

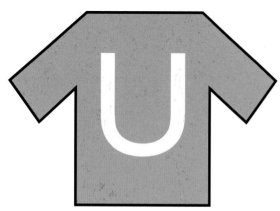

UEFA

UEFA is the governing body of European football. Created in 1954, it united the football associations of Belgium, France and Italy, and promoted both national (European Championships) and club (Europa League and UEFA Champions League) competitions.

The UEFA Champions League is the premier club competition, with Real Madrid winning it a record number of times.

Unbelievable

In a game in 1945 between Arsenal and Moscow, a dense fog suddenly rolled onto the pitch. The referee didn't want to reschedule the game because the visiting team had travelled so far, but things soon got out of hand. An Arsenal player was sent off the field, but sneaked back on and wasn't spotted in the fog. The Russians were suspected of having 15 players on the pitch instead of 11. The Arsenal goalie ran into the goalpost and was knocked unconscious so a spectator ran onto the pitch and filled in for the rest of the game.

Utility players

Utility players can comfortably play in defence, midfield or attack. Between 2004 and 2008, Sheffield Wednesday's Lee Bullen played in each of the 11 different positions, including goalkeeper.

Vuvuzela

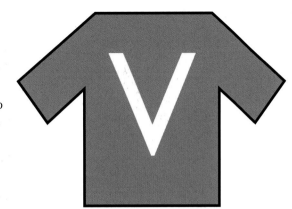

The vuvuzela (a long, colourful, plastic horn) achieved notoriety during the 2010 World Cup in South Africa, when players and spectators complained about the noise it created. Many English clubs have banned the instrument. But the vuvuzela was not the first instrument to be banned – wooden rattles were banned in the 1970s because they were thought to pose a danger in the hands of hooligans.

Other, more bizarre, objects that have been banned include giant inflatable bananas – a craze spread by Manchester City fans, who adopted them in honour of their striker Imre Varadi (nicknamed "Imre Banana") – and dead chickens. A Manchester City fan was banned in 1995 from bringing dead chickens into City's Maine Road ground. He liked to celebrate his team's goals by swinging the birds around his head.

Viewers

The first ever televised football match was between Arsenal and Arsenal Reserves in 1937, when there were only a few thousand televisions around. The 2010 World Cup final was watched by 700 million viewers worldwide.

Volley

A volley is when a player kicks the ball while it's in the air (and hasn't touched the ground or bounced since the last player touched it).

Women's football

Women's football is not a modern development. In the 1920s, it was attracting large crowds. In fact, a crowd of 53,000 was recorded at a women's match at Everton's Goodison Park. The FA responded by introducing a ban on women's football at League grounds for the next 50 years.

World Cup

The World Cup is the premier international football tournament. It was first played in Uruguay in 1930, and its final stage has been held every four years since then (except in 1942 and 1946, due to World War II).

Brazil has won the most World Cup competitions and is the only team to qualify for every finals. The record number of World Cup goals scored by a single player is 15 by Brazil's Ronaldo.

Whistle

Referees use a whistle to help control matches – to stop, start or restart play. In the early years of football, referees indicated their decisions by waving a handkerchief.

The first referee's whistle was introduced in 1878 by Joseph Hudson, who had also introduced whistles into the Metropolitan Police force after winning a competition to come up with the best way of attracting people's attention.

Imagine if a similar competition took place today – we'd probably have the referee tweeting decisions from his mobile phone. Bring back the hanky!

Xmas Day matches

On 25 December 1914, 100,000 British and German troops along the Western Front stopped fighting each other, and soldiers from both sides left their trenches and met in no-man's land to exchange gifts of beer and plum pudding. Several games of football broke out. The only recorded result was for a match that the Germans won 3-2.

At 8.30am on Boxing Day, ceremonial pistol shots announced the resumption of the Great War, in which more than nine million people would eventually lose their lives.

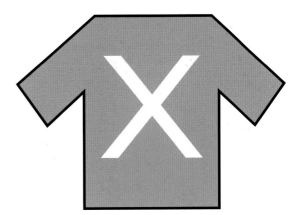

The last time that most Football League clubs played on Christmas Day was in 1957, when 38 matches took place. After that, the number dwindled because fans preferred to stay at home. The last match played on Christmas Day was in 1965, when Blackpool (dressed appropriately in tangerine) defeated Blackburn Rovers 4-2 in a First Division match in front of more than 20,000 spectators.

MeXico

Fifty-two-year-old Pedro Gatica cycled nearly 5,000 kilometres from his home in Argentina to Mexico for the 1986 World Cup, only to find, on arrival, that he couldn't afford to get in. While he was haggling for a ticket, thieves stole his bike.

Yellow and red cards

The use of yellow cards to caution players for bad behaviour on the pitch and red cards to send them off was first introduced during the 1970 World Cup in Mexico. The idea came just four years earlier, when referee Ken Aston watched traffic lights change from amber to red on his way home from Wembley Stadium during the 1966 World Cup.

Now there's an idea!

Red and yellow cards are a simple system, but mistakes can happen. In the 2006 World Cup, referee Graham Poll forgot to send Croatia's Josip Simunic off the pitch after awarding him a second yellow card. However, he did eventually send the Croatian off when he picked up his third yellow card of the match! That's more cards than some players get in their whole career – former England Captain Gary Lineker (dubbed "Mr Nice Guy") played for Everton, Leicester City, Tottenham Hotspurs, and Barcelona without once receiving a yellow or red card.

Zaire

When Zaire (now the Democratic Republic of the Congo) advanced to the tournament stage of the 1974 World Cup, things didn't go as planned. After losing 9-0 to Yugoslavia, the players were told that, if they lost to Brazil by more than three goals, they wouldn't be allowed back home. As the Brazilians prepared to take a free kick, things were looking bad, so defender Mwepu Ilunga charged at the players and kicked the ball out of the way. He was given a yellow card, but in the end Zaire only lost 3-0 and all was well.

Zizinho and Zizou

You might think that Brazilian footballer Zizinho would be unique in helping his team reach the final of the World Cup (in 1950) in his home country, receiving the "Golden Ball" as top player in the tournament and having two zeds in his name. But then along comes Zinedine Zidane (nickname Zizou). He achieved the same feat by reaching the World Cup final in France in 1998 and winning the "Golden Ball". Zidane also helped France secure victory in the final – its first World Cup win.

Talking of "Golden balls", this was the nickname given to David Beckham (one-time teammate of Zizou). Other nicknames for great players include: "Rei" ("King") for Pele, "Pelusa" ("Dishevelled One") for Maradona and the "Non-flying Dutchman" for Dennis Bergkamp (because of his fear of flying). Who will be next on the list of great players?

Could it be you?